# THE ULTIMATE
# PROFIT PLAYBOOK

AMERICAN DREAM
INVESTING®

# THE ULTIMATE
# PROFIT PLAYBOOK

## A SIMPLIFIED, STEP-BY-STEP GUIDE TO PICKING WINNERS IN THE STOCK MARKET

By Karl Kaufman

Supplemental material is available as a companion to this edition

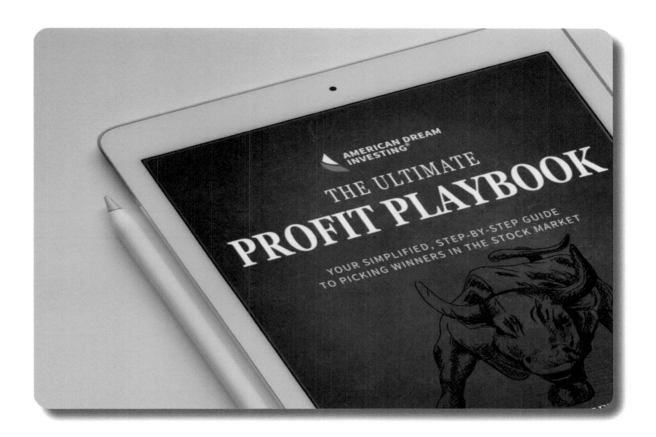

Scan the QR Code above with your
smartphone camera or visit:

## UltimateProfitPlaybook.com/bonus

Left to Right: Karl, Richard and Jonathan Kaufman

Dedicated to the memory of
**Richard H. Kaufman**

"May the work I have done speak for me."

# About The Author

Karl Kaufman has years of experience showing others how he makes money in the stock market. He gives seminars and hosts talks at universities, investment clubs and financial events throughout the country.

As a contributor for Forbes.com, he writes about money and the markets with the individual investor in mind. His articles and interviews with luminaries such as Tony Robbins, Peter Diamandis and Jeffrey Gundlach have been read by more than a million people worldwide. He has also appeared in Kiplinger, Bloomberg, U.S. News & World Report and Jim Cramer's TheStreet.

Karl graduated from Cornell University and began his career as a stock market data analyst. He passed the Series 65 exam, required to become a financial advisor, using that knowledge to become a better investor. Rather than managing other people's money, he's focused on teaching investors to think differently about the stock market.

## A Legacy of Successful Investing

Karl's father, Richard Kaufman, was an individual investor who tripled his net worth during retirement. Richard's proprietary methodology, developed over four decades, was taught to Karl, who uses those same tactics to make financial gains to this day.

Karl used that philosophy to launch American Dream Investing in 2016. It serves as a voice for the individual investor, providing clear and actionable tools to build wealth. With American Dream Investing, members get access to proven strategies from multiple generations of successful investors.

Karl lives in Boca Raton, Florida, with his wife Rachel and two children, Max and Raina.

To request permissions or for bulk purchases please contact:
info@americandreaminvesting.com

ISBN:
Paperback: 978-1-955230-00-1
eBook: 978-1-955230-01-8

First edition: October 2021
Printed in the United States of America

Library of Congress Control Number: 2021909894

Editor: Jonathan Kaufman
Editor: Lauren Fogel

DISCLAIMER: Past performance is no guarantee of future results. All information in this book is for educational purposes only. Investment information is provided without consideration of your financial sophistication, financial situation, investing time horizon or risk tolerance. You should consult with a professional where appropriate.

The information in this book was correct at the time of publication; the Author does not assume any liability for loss or damage caused by errors or omissions. Your capital is at risk when you invest - you can lose some or all of your money. Never risk more than you can afford to lose.

PLEASE REVIEW OUR FULL DISCLOSURE AT THE END OF THIS BOOK PRIOR TO MAKING ANY INVESTMENT DECISIONS.

Bullhorn Books
1200 N Federal Highway, Suite 200
Boca Raton, FL 33432

Bullhornbooks.com
Americandreaminvesting.com

# Table of Contents

*A lone amateur built the ark;*
*a large group of professionals built the Titanic.*

- UNKNOWN

# Introduction

*How can ordinary investors achieve extraordinary returns?*

Financial professionals have tried to stack the deck against individual investors like us. It's in their best interest to keep things as confusing as possible so that most people give up control of their hard-earned money and utilize their services.

**But who's making money off of your money?**

Years ago, the best way to get exposure to the stock market and reap some of its profits was to let the professionals handle your money, usually with a fund, a stockbroker or a wealth manager. They would sell a product to earn extra commissions while charging exorbitant fees for that privilege.

Why was that? Was it to keep the average person from joining the profit party? Was it so that some "professionals" could justify their existence despite a sub-par track record?

I was in the same boat! My portfolio was mostly filled with mutual funds, and I wasn't reaching my financial goals. I considered managing my investments myself, but there was so much information available that I was confused and didn't know where to start.

Finally, I got fed up with accepting average results from the mutual fund managers who controlled my financial destiny and took matters (and my money) into my own hands...

I started by understanding the fundamentals of analyzing a company and its effect on stock price movements. I read everything I could get my hands on about the stock market.

I learned from the experience of successful investors, including my father, who tripled his net worth in retirement despite being a scientist by trade. When he passed away in January 2020, I assumed the role of managing his multimillion-dollar portfolio, guiding it to a **47.49% gain in 2020**.

In my years of investing experience, I haven't found a straightforward strategy guide designed for an individual investor. That's why I created this Playbook: to keep my investment strategies and critical thinking techniques in one organized place. I wanted a resource that I could turn to whenever I consider investing in a stock.

# Don't Settle For Average

One of the biggest blunders an investor can make is blindly accepting average results in the stock market.

For example, standard financial advice dictates that diversification is the key to limiting risk. I believe the opposite: over diversifying still exposes investors to market risk while also limiting their upside. There are hundreds of companies in a typical index or ETF that I wouldn't buy individually; why would I want to own them as part of a fund (and pay fees to the fund manager on top of that)?

American Dream Investing's concentrated portfolio has gained 569% over the last ten years, from 1/1/2011 to 1/1/2021. For perspective, a $500,000 investment would have grown to **$3.345 million** over that period, without paying fees to fund managers or advisors. The only fees paid were trading commissions, which are now mostly a thing of the past!

In comparison, a diversified index fund that tracks the S&P 500 is up 267% over the same period, not including fees. That $500,000 investment would have turned into a $1.835 million portfolio. Not bad, but wouldn't you rather have $3.345 million?

# The Power Of The Individual Investor

Individual investors hold an advantage over professionals. Rules and regulations handcuff mutual funds and financial advisors, whereas we can construct our portfolio however we see fit. The pressure of performance continually weighs on funds and advisors; we only need to make enough profits to support our lifestyle!

Let's put our entrepreneurial hat on for a minute and consider each stock in our portfolio as if it were a business we owned. We would know a great deal about the inner workings of the business and those who were responsible for running it.

In this Playbook, I've provided step-by-step instructions and commentary along the way to show how I research the inner workings of the stocks in my portfolio that have helped me beat the market.

## THIS BOOK IS ORGANIZED TO SHOW HOW I:

▸ Find a prospective stock to invest in

▸ Know exactly which numbers to prioritize and where to find them

▸ Develop critical thinking that gives me an edge over the market

▸ Use unconventional web search ideas to uncover information ignored by most investors (these clues can be the key to spotting opportunities)

I'm passionate about sharing my knowledge about the stock market. I was inspired to write this book to illustrate a method that has worked for my father and me. Maybe it will work for you too!

In life, there are typically no shortcuts to success. However, we have used the techniques outlined in this Playbook to make our time spent researching companies more efficient, help keep us organized and improve our confidence in our investments.

Here's to many happy returns,

Karl Kaufman

# How To Use This Playbook

When most people hear the words "Income Statement" and "Balance Sheet," their eyes immediately glaze over, and they move on to shinier objects. We've attempted to simplify the process of scanning these financial reports to quickly find what we're looking for without being bored or ignoring this essential process.

After all, as a shareholder, we own a piece of this business - why not try to understand how the company's management is spending our money?

Following the Playbook steps focuses attention on using fundamental analysis to project a stock's future price action. My team and I use these methods in our research, and I'd like to thank them for their ongoing contributions to this work.

Throughout the Playbook, you'll find several call-out sections marked "ADI Edge." These are some of American Dream Investing's next-level thinking about the market, which we've used to achieve annual returns of 20.93% over the last ten years (compared to 13.88% for the S&P 500).

You'll also find a list of some of the direct resources used to construct this Playbook, as well as a Glossary, which you can refer to if you come across any unfamiliar terms. We prefer to use Morningstar.com for research.

You can utilize this Playbook fully or partially and still gain useful insights. The real trick is this: as you go through the Playbook, you'll start to see meaningful trends. You'll have "A-ha" moments where you'll discover a critical point that signifies that an investment could be worthwhile.

In this Playbook, we provide guidance and demonstrate easy ways to find the information investors need. We also offer you areas to work on your ideas to find insights into which direction a company is heading.

You'll find additional note pages at the end of the Playbook for sections that may require more research or to jot down your ideas. You can also print out relevant sections as needed for each stock you're researching.

# PART ONE

# Shopping Around

"

*Buy a stock the way you would buy a house. Understand and like it such that you'd be content to own it in the absence of any market.*

WARREN BUFFETT

# Stock Selection

Selecting the right stocks is the foundation of portfolio management. Once we hone in on an appealing company, the next critical component is understanding how to allocate our investment dollars to maximize our returns and limit our risk.

When selecting a company to buy shares in, there are several chief questions we ask ourselves. In no particular order, they are:

1. What are my goals for the investment?
   *(Holding long-term, income from dividends, making short-term trades)*

   _____

   _____

   _____

2. What is the % allocation that this holding will represent of my:

   **a.** Total Investments: _____

   **b.** Total Stock Portfolio: _____

3. How much time will I devote to finding a good company and following it?

   _____

4. What industry/sector is this company in?

   *(Circle the industry)*

   | | | |
   |---|---|---|
   | Financials | Energy | Consumer Discretionary |
   | Industrials | Utilities | Consumer Staples |
   | Technology | Healthcare | Communication Services |
   | Real Estate | Materials | |

5. Does this company pay a dividend? If so, what is its yield?

_____

_____

_____

6. Who are its competitors?

_____

_____

_____

_____

_____

_____

7. What kind of potential risks do I foresee facing this company? Examples to consider:

- **Exxon Mobil**: What could happen to the stock price if the price of oil plummets?
- **PepsiCo**: What would happen to PepsiCo if there were a push away from sugar and towards healthier snacks and drinks?
- What happens to bank stocks when interest rates go down?

_____

_____

_____

_____

_____

_____

_____

_____

_____

_____

_____

8. What type of company is this, based on Peter Lynch's categories? Lynch detailed the stages of a business in his bestselling book *One Up On Wall Street* on pg. 112, which we've summarized below. *(Circle the category)*

| | | |
|---|---|---|
| Stalwart | Fast Grower | Turnaround |
| Slow Grower | Cyclical | Asset Play |

a. **Stalwart** - Huge companies that don't grow too fast in the short-term but have solid prospects for long-term growth. Traits would be increasing dividends, excellent cash flow, and limited debt.

b. **Slow Grower** - Similar sized company to Stalwart, but its fast-growth years are well behind it.

c. **Fast Grower** - Usually early phase companies with rapid growth along with a potentially volatile stock price. Many Fast Growers do not have significant earnings, but the stock price is traded up based on potential earnings and continued innovation. Breaking news relating to their operations can dramatically affect the share price.

d. **Cyclical** - Companies whose profits rise and fall based on economic cycles. For example, when the economy is booming, the automotive industry tends to do well, as consumers have more money to upgrade their vehicles. When there's a recession, companies in the consumer staples sector, such as those that sell cigarettes or food, usually do well since people always need to restock these items.

e. **Turnaround** - These companies have been battered down or depressed, and no growth or even negative growth has left them in poor shape. Think airline and travel/leisure companies throughout the COVID-19 pandemic. Often, the company will bring in a new CEO to try and turn around its fortunes.

f. **Asset Play** - By looking at and understanding a company's Balance Sheet, we may discover hidden or under-reported assets that add extra value to its earnings potential. We may believe the market has not correctly priced its actual value based on these additional assets.

9. How well do I know the company and understand its products or services?

_____

_____

_____

_____

# Stock Summary

This information is available on most financial news sites.
We prefer to use Morningstar.com

Company Name

Stock Ticker

Share Price

$

52 Week

High

$

-

Low

$

Market Cap

$

Dividend

$

Dividend Yield

EPS

$

Next Earnings Date

P/E Ratio

# Notes

# PART TWO
# Detective Work

"

*Average investors can become experts in their own field and can pick winning stocks as effectively as Wall Street professionals by doing just a little research.*

PETER LYNCH

# Income Statement

The Income Statement (also known as the Profit/Loss Statement or P&L) shows the Revenue and Expenses of a business for a defined period, such as a quarter or fiscal year. Put simply:

 How much does a company need to spend in order to generate sales?

We hear a lot about top-line vs. bottom-line results when companies release their earnings reports. The top-line of an Income Statement shows the total **Revenue (sales)** for that period. After subtracting all the Expenses, we're left with **Net Income (PROFIT)** on the bottom line of the Income Statement. As far as we're concerned, we want companies to show us something good on the bottom line!

Note that earnings can be negative for newer businesses (typically less than ten years old). These companies tend to focus more on using cash to fuel growth instead of generating consistent profits. For instance, it took nearly ten years for Amazon to post its first profitable year.

This Playbook specifically addresses more mature companies with reliable data and solid financial health.

We look for trends over a five-year time frame as they progress in an upward, downward or flat direction. We like to see positive growth in a company's **Revenues** and **Net Income** (also known as **Earnings**) while seeing its **Cost of Goods Sold** decrease if possible.

Typically, companies must spend more to increase Revenue, which then decreases Earnings. If the company can generate more Revenue while limiting Expenses and growing Earnings, it's a strong indication of efficient management.

Fill in the appropriate historical data for a company by looking for the 'Financials' section on any financial news website. For analysis on this page, it's best to find five years of data to get a comprehensive view of the trends.

## Revenues

| 20___ | 20___ | 20___ | 20___ | 20___ |
|---|---|---|---|---|
|  |  |  |  |  |

## Cost of Goods Sold

| 20___ | 20___ | 20___ | 20___ | 20___ |
|---|---|---|---|---|
|  |  |  |  |  |

## Net Income

| 20___ | 20___ | 20___ | 20___ | 20___ |
|---|---|---|---|---|
|  |  |  |  |  |

# Balance Sheet

If the Income Statement is like a moving picture, showing financial results over a specific period, the Balance Sheet is a snapshot in time. It shows us what the company owns (**Assets**), what the company owes in debt (**Liabilities**), and what the company owes to us, the shareholder (**Equity**), right now.

*As its name suggests, the Balance Sheet must be balanced. This simple equation is:*

Total Assets = Total Liabilities + Total Equity

A company's Balance Sheet is usually listed under the 'Financials' section at a financial website. It's useful to look at the Balance Sheet to see how much debt the company owes.

If a company has too much debt in the Liabilities section, they may have problems paying dividends and sustaining or expanding their operations. Ballooning debt could raise a red flag for current or potential investors, negatively affecting the stock.

Now, debt is not necessarily bad—companies frequently borrow money to grow, and growth is a good thing! We're interested in two metrics to decipher the company's short-term and long-term debts.

The first exercise is to calculate the **Current Ratio**. This ratio is an easy way to gauge a company's short-term liquidity, critical to its flexibility and solvency. If we look at **Current Assets** (assets that can be sold within one year) divided by **Current Liabilities** (debts due within one year), we can see how management operates on both sides of the Balance Sheet in the short-term. Ideally, the resulting number would be at least 1 and between 1.3 and 2, meaning the company's short-term assets are enough to cover their short-term liabilities. We most likely won't have to worry about bankruptcy in the near term.

The importance of the Current Ratio varies depending on the industry. Therefore, we usually compare similar companies within the same sector.

## Current Assets ÷ Current Liabilities = Current Ratio

|  | 20__ | 20__ | 20__ | 20__ | 20__ |
|---|---|---|---|---|---|
| Current Assets |  |  |  |  |  |
| Current Liabilities |  |  |  |  |  |
| Current Ratio |  |  |  |  |  |

In *One Up On Wall Street*, Peter Lynch has a clever way of finding insights within the Balance Sheet. He places more emphasis on long-term debt by calculating **Net Cash Per Share**. The formula is as follows:

$$\frac{(\text{Cash and Total Short Term Equivalents} + \text{Total Short Term Investments}) - \text{Long Term Debt}}{\text{Shares Outstanding}}$$

$$= \text{Net Cash Per Share}$$

The higher the number, the better. By focusing on how much Net Cash, if any, is available per share, we're seeking hidden value in the company. This formula has enabled us to find undervalued gems!

| | 20___ | 20___ | 20___ | 20___ | 20___ |
|---|---|---|---|---|---|
| Cash and Total Short Term Equivalents | | | | | |
| Total Short Term Investments | | | | | |
| Long Term Debt | | | | | |
| Common Shares Outstanding * | | | | | |

Calculations:

| | 20___ | 20___ | 20___ | 20___ | 20___ |
|---|---|---|---|---|---|
| Net Cash Per Share | | | | | |

*Shares Outstanding can be found easily on Morningstar.com on the company's main Quote page under the "Short Interest" tab.*

# Statement Of Cash Flows

> Profits are an opinion; cash is a fact.

Cash is king. Profits are all well and good, but you can't spend profits! While it's true that a company without profits won't have a lot of cash, a profitable company without extra cash won't be growing very much.

Revenue and earnings get all the attention, but the most important thing we look at when analyzing an investment is the company's **Free Cash Flow (FCF)**. FCF is the cash a company generates after accounting for cash needed to support Operations (payroll, sales, expenses), Investments (buying or selling fixed assets and equipment) and Financing (borrowing/raising money, distributions to shareholders).

Unscrupulous management can "massage" earnings through creative accounting. It requires some sleuthing to uncover where the company is hiding the truth. Even the Statement of Cash Flows can be manipulated depending on how the company categorizes its Operating, Investing or Financing Cash.

Free Cash Flow, though, is hard to hide and very useful to shareholders. If a company is growing Free Cash Flow over time, management has more opportunity to buy back shares or give that cash back to shareholders via dividends. The company can also use that cash to fuel internal growth or explore acquisition targets.

| | 20__ | 20__ | 20__ | 20__ | 20__ |
|---|---|---|---|---|---|
| Free Cash Flow | | | | | |

Free Cash Flow can be easily found on YahooFinance.com under the "Financials → Cash Flow" section

# Dividends

Do you know the only thing that gives me pleasure?
It's to see my dividends coming in.

- JOHN D. ROCKEFELLER

Dividends are like a paycheck from a company as a reward for being a shareholder. The best part: we don't have to get dressed for work, sit in rush hour traffic, or pretend to be busy as the boss walks past our desk. *We're* the boss, and we get to give the annual or quarterly performance report to see if the company is worth keeping!

Better yet, if we find the right company, we'll receive a raise each year that outpaces inflation.

The **Dividend Yield** is the first metric to investigate. Yield is the percentage of the stock price that's paid out to shareholders annually. By understanding yield, we can measure the return on investment we'd get from a stock without having to sell it.

As of this writing, Home Depot's yearly dividend is $6.60 per share, and its share price is $317.30. Divide the dividend by the share price ($6.60 / $317.30), and we'll see that Home Depot's dividend yield is 2.08%. Since Home Depot pays a quarterly dividend, we'll receive a payment of $1.65 per share every three months as a shareholder.

# DIVIDENDS

The dividend is paid on what is known as the **"Ex-Dividend"** date. On that date, the dividend is taken from the share price and paid to shareholders who've owned the stock at least one day before the ex-dividend date.

Assuming Home Depot's ex-dividend date is September 2nd, we'll receive $1.65 per share as long as we owned the stock on or before September 1st. If the stock closes the trading day on September 1st at $331.65, that $1.65 dividend payment gets taken out of the share price. The next day, September 2nd, Home Depot will start trading at $330.00 ($331.65 - $1.65 = $330.00).

The share price and yield have an inverse relationship: as the price rises, the yield goes down and vice versa. If Home Depot's share price climbs to $340, the yield would now be 1.94% ($6.60 / $340).

When interest rates are low, dividend stocks are more in favor. Income investors won't be satisfied with low-yielding Treasury bills and often buy dividend stocks. Ironically, this causes the stock price to rise and the yield to fall.

Many investors fall into what's known as a "yield trap" and buy a stock only because it has a high yield. The high yield might be a warning sign that something is fundamentally wrong with the company.

For instance, AT&T shareholders who owned the stock due to its 7% yield received a rude awakening in May 2021. The company announced it would cut its dividend payment by nearly 50% after ill-advised acquisitions and 5G infrastructure costs contributed to expanding debt. The high dividend payment was no longer sustainable.

# Protecting Our Paycheck

Though we don't work for this company, we do need to do some work for ourselves to ensure the business can sustain paying us this "salary."

The next number to look for is the **Dividend Payout Ratio.** This ratio measures the percentage of the company's earnings paid as dividends. Though the ratio is reported on financial websites, it's easy and valuable to know how to calculate this: **divide the dividends paid by the company's Net Income.**

A good rule of thumb is the lower the ratio, the better. The company is not paying too much out of its cash supply to maintain the dividend and can support it should there be a temporary decline in earnings.

Just as the best investors don't subscribe to a specific philosophy, there are no hard, fast rules here. By understanding the company well and knowing that they purposely maintain a particular Payout Ratio, we can rely on the company to continue to pay the dividend.

One of the stocks in our portfolio has a Payout Ratio of around 80%, which is considered very high. We know that management targets this number and consistently keeps it around this level, so we're not concerned about the dividend. Other investors might skip over this company solely because the Payout Ratio does not conform to their rulebook.

Finally, we want to find a company that is growing its dividend payments. How many years in a row has the company increased its dividend? We look at the historical track record of dividend payouts to understand how often they grow the dividend and what percentage it gets raised. This number is known as the **Dividend Growth Rate**. We're looking for a raise that outpaces inflation, at least.

If they've continuously raised the dividend annually for 25 years, the stock is considered a Dividend Aristocrat. Once a company is on that list, they need to continue to raise the dividend to qualify for inclusion.

Compile the numbers concerning the dividends in a table and go through a short exercise to calculate the dividend's growth percentage for the past five years. You can find this information on Morningstar.com by finding the company's stock and then clicking on the "Dividends" tab.

| | 20___ | 20___ | 20___ | 20___ | 20___ |
|---|---|---|---|---|---|
| Trailing Dividend Yield (%) | | | | | |
| Payout Ratio (%) | | | | | |
| Dividend Per Share | | | | | |

NOW, USING A CALCULATOR, WE SIMPLY:

- ▶ Take the most recent year of Dividends paid per share, then
- ▶ Subtract the prior year's Dividend payment
- ▶ Take that result and divide it by the prior year's Dividend payment
- ▶ Multiply that number by 100, and we have our annual Dividend Growth Rate!

Here's an example of how to calculate the Growth Rate, followed by a table to fill out.

Referencing the table below with sample data, we will calculate five years of Dividend Growth Rate. Here are the steps as laid out above:

1. $3.00

2. $3.00 - $2.80 = (0.2)

3. 0.2 / $2.80 = (.0714)

4. .0714 x 100 = **7.14%**

Dividend Growth Rate from 2019 - 2020

| | 2015 | 2016 | 2017 | 2018 | 2019 | 2020 |
|---|---|---|---|---|---|---|
| Dividend Per Share | $2.30 | $2.50 | $2.65 | $2.70 | $2.80 | $3.00 |
| Growth Rate (%) | _____ | 8.70% | 6.00% | 1.89% | 3.70% | **7.14%** |

*In the table above, please note that the 2015 Growth Rate % row is empty because we would need 2014's Dividend Payment to calculate this data.*

This exercise helps us get a broader understanding of how the company raises dividends over the last five years. We then compare it to our other investments or other dividend-paying companies within the same industry to determine whether the company is growing its dividend at an acceptable rate.

| | 20___ | 20___ | 20___ | 20___ | 20___ | 20___ |
|---|---|---|---|---|---|---|
| Dividend Per Share | | | | | | |
| Growth Rate (%) | _____ | | | | | |

In a volatile market environment, it's vital to limit downside risk. Owning quality stocks with a consistent record of paying dividends protects our portfolio, especially during bear markets (when stocks fall 20% from their highs).

Companies with strong Balance Sheets and a history of committing to dividend payments can ensure we collect income regardless of market conditions.

Now, what happens when we get paid the dividend? Do we automatically reinvest it in the same stock?

Here's why we don't automatically reinvest the dividend: it limits our control over our cash. We use dividend payments to generate cash flow within the portfolio.

Cash gives us options. We could accumulate that cash in the account, patiently hold on to it, and wait for temporary dips in the market and buy on weakness. We could use it to purchase a different stock if the dividend-paying company is too expensive at the moment. We can use the cash to buy a new car, pay for college or take a fun family vacation.

In this low-yield environment, our portfolio consists of several high-yielding dividend stocks that act like an annuity. The best part: we don't have to hand over a chunk of money to an insurance company or worry about an early withdrawal fee. We always like to maintain full control over our money; steady dividend-paying stocks give us that ability!

# PART THREE

# Gaining An Edge

"

*The most contrarian thing of all is not to oppose the crowd but to think for yourself.*

PETER THIEL

# Management

Here are a few ways we think critically about management:

Even if we think the business is a well-run organization, we want to consider whether management is, and will remain, shareholder-friendly.

Some companies believe the dividend is sacred and will do whatever is necessary to protect and raise it. Share buybacks are another way of returning capital to shareholders in a tax-efficient manner and could be a sign from management that they believe the stock is undervalued.

If they're not engaged in buybacks or dividends, what do they do with cash flow? Do they fuel growth by investing in research and development? Do they use cash for smart mergers or acquisitions, buying relevant companies within their industry to enhance their business strategy? Think of Pepsi buying Quaker Oats; Pepsi was able to expand its product line into healthier options that complemented its brand.

AOL and Time Warner's deal is an example of a poor management decision. At the time, AOL was a hot tech stock in the communications industry, while Time Warner was an old-guard media company. There weren't many synergies there, and the deal was commonly regarded as a disaster for both companies' shareholders.

We also check management's compensation. If it's tied to company earnings, it will benefit shareholders as it incentivizes management to grow profits.

When it comes to insider transactions, it's easy to think that insider selling could be a bad sign. However, it's not a very useful or accurate analysis tool, as we never know why the company's leadership is selling. The CFO's daughter could be heading off to college next fall, or the Chairman of the Board might need a new yacht.

On the other hand, insider buying is an excellent sign of what management thinks of the company's prospects. There are many reasons why someone would sell their stock, but there's only really one reason why they would buy -- they think the stock is going up!

Another way we subjectively analyze a company is by examining whether we believe management is trustworthy. This requires experience, instinct and intuition. We listen to earnings conference calls to see how they answer questions towards the end with the Q & A section. We ignore the softball questions and focus on how they answer the more challenging questions.

Media interviews can be insightful, which is one reason why we watch CNBC. We look closely at body language as CEOs field difficult questions -- can we spot them squirming as they're telling a lie?

We also check reviews on Glassdoor.com to gain insight into what former and current employees think of management. We'll get an idea if the company's workers approve of the CEO.

As with any review site, some comments should be taken with a grain of salt, as disgruntled ex-employees have a platform to air their opinions anonymously. However, if we notice a pattern, it could signify that the company's employees don't have confidence in their management.

---

Understanding a company on a structural level can lead to further insights into its efficiencies.

Consider this: in 2006, Apple employed 17,000 people. By 2019, that number grew eightfold to 137,000. However, the number of Vice Presidents within the organization less than doubled, from 50 to 96.

Because of this leadership structure, each division head must take a more collaborative approach with their whole team. This strategy allows for more high-level training within each department, leading to greater efficiencies and innovation.

---

Use the following space to write down notes and insights concerning management. Dig into the archives to find CNBC interviews, company conference calls, and articles about the company's executives.

# Notes On Management

# In The News

Breaking news and current events have a direct impact on the direction of a company's share price. We set Google news alerts and watch CNBC for developing stories that may affect our holdings.

The CEO could be involved in a scandal; a drug company may fail in Phase III trials; there could be a positive announcement or an earnings beat that sends the stock soaring. Any event, large or small, can have an immediate impact on the stock.

When news hits, investors try to price in how the information could affect future earnings. We're often able to buy more shares at a discount when the market has overreacted to a story.

Why not take advantage when others get spooked over something that may only have a short-term effect on the stock? When we've done our due diligence and still believe in the company's long-term story, we often add to our position at a lower price.

Many experienced investors know the wise lesson of "taking emotion out of your decisions." Even beginner investors have likely heard it at some point. Falling victim to emotions leads to the most irresponsible and harmful investment decisions, which is why we've devoted an entire chapter to it later in the Playbook.

## Hidden in Plain "Site"

We like to be creative with our web detective skills. Breaking news is significant but is delivered at the same time to millions of other investors. By searching on Google using creative keywords, we sometimes find surprising, underreported stories that could impact the business. More importantly, these stories might be ignored by other investors.

We start a more in-depth search with phrases that include the company name and keywords such as:

"Patent applications for (Company Name)"
"(Company Name) acquisition targets"
"New developments by (Company Name)"
"(Company Name) making strides in the market"

Another underutilized technique is to look through job postings. Is the company expanding its workforce, and in what departments? This could provide hints into where the company is targeting growth.

ADDITIONAL SEARCH TERMS:

merger, acquisition, development, dividend, offering, target, share, compete, market, risk, growth, decline, innovation, technology, earnings, strategy, moat

Record relevant information from two or more recent articles using the space provided on the following page.

Article One:

*(Name of Article)*

Notes:

*(New Offerings, Price Targets, Additional Relevant Information)*

Statistics:

*(FCF, Dividend, Guidance/Earnings, Other Statistics of Interest)*

Implications:

*(Where is the company headed? Competition, Market Share)*

---

Article Two:

*(Name of Article)*

Notes:

*(New Offerings, Price Targets, Additional Relevant Information)*

Statistics:

*(FCF, Dividend, Guidance/Earnings, Other Statistics of Interest)*

Implications:

*(Where is the company headed? Competition, Market Share)*

# Competition & The Moat

When evaluating a company's growth prospects, we always consider its Market Share relative to its competitors.

We aim to fully understand a company and its place within its entire industry. Industry leaders often grow complacent and find themselves replaced by more innovative competition.

Think of the moat surrounding a castle: it serves as a buffer between the building and any invaders. A company's Economic Moat refers to its ability to sustain a competitive advantage over competitors to protect its long-term profits and Market Share.

Competition can be of value when it drives the company towards further innovation and efficiency.

Our research can help us anticipate this by:

▶ Understanding management

▶ Looking at the company's track record

▶ Staying up to date on new developments

▶ Learning where the company is focusing its Research & Development dollars

Investors who understand the dynamics within an industry can spot areas where a market leader is vulnerable or has enough of an advantage to withstand a competitor's best shot.

Think of the competitive advantage Google has for selling ads. It'd be hard to imagine many advertisers diverting their ad spend to Bing or Yahoo as their impact would be minimal compared to Google's platform. However, suppose Apple decides to switch its default search engine away from Google and develop a competing product. In that case, Google's future earnings might be drastically reduced if Apple limits access to Google's platform for its billions of users.

On a deeper level of analysis, by looking at Google's EPS and profit margin, we see that their margins are incredible because of the service that they sell. Ad space on the internet requires less overhead than producing or selling a tangible product.

That gives them a comfortable cushion to withstand such a move by a competitive partner. In a way, it serves as the glue that keeps the partnership intact despite the competitive areas that these two companies operate.

Remember that leadership changes, times and tastes evolve, and patents and contracts expire; the business cycle is in constant flux. By staying up-to-date with the companies we invest in, we can start get a good idea if a company's moat begins to shrink.

We've created a "One Page Stock Analysis" worksheet directly following this section. Here are the steps to analyze the competitive landscape:

# STEP 1:

Start by finding the company's direct competitors. Utilize Morningstar.com: under the "Stock Analysis" tab, determine two competitors, ensuring that their market caps are of a similar size.

# STEP 2:

Identify key attributes of each competitor. What is this company known for? What is its unique advantage in the marketplace, if any?

## STEP 3:

Find relevant information, including current and future developments within the company. Could it be on the verge of a breakthrough, such as launching a new product or applying for a patent? If so, how would that change the landscape of the industry? Keep in mind that competitors may lose market share when patents expire, they lose subscribers, or an upstart enters the market.

## STEP 4:

Next, do an abridged financial comparison using the table on the "One Page Stock Analysis" worksheet on the following page. Collecting this data allows us to assess the financial conditions of the competition.

## STEP 5:

Let's synthesize all of the information we've analyzed to reach a conclusion about the competitive landscape:

▶ What kind of story do the financial numbers tell?

▶ Have we found interesting articles in our research that can provide context for the market landscape?

This detective work will serve as a great foundation to process all of the work we have done. We may even find that a competitor has more going for it than our initial company of interest. In that case, perhaps it deserves our investment dollars instead of our original target.

# One Page Stock Analysis

| Company Name | Stock Ticker | Share Price |
|---|---|---|
|  |  | $ |

| Market Cap. | P/E Ratio | EPS |
|---|---|---|
| $ |  | $ |

## Business Insights

**Short Business Description**

**Major Products/Services**
▶
▶
▶
▶

**Advantages Against Competitors**
▶
▶
▶
▶

**Analysis of Current News**

**Thoughts on Future Growth**

## Financials

|  | 20___ | 20___ | 20___ |
|---|---|---|---|
| Net Income |  |  |  |
| Current Ratio |  |  |  |
| Free Cash Flow |  |  |  |
| Yield (%) |  |  |  |
| Dividend Growth Rate (%) |  |  |  |

## Conclusion

**Insights from Financials**
▶
▶
▶

**Insights from Research**
▶
▶
▶

**Is this a worthwhile investment and at what price?**

# When To Sell A Stock

Buying and holding a stock is straightforward enough. The trickiest part of investing for most people is knowing when to sell.

Here are a few reasons why we would sell a stock:

### The theory behind why we bought the stock changed

Perhaps, during our ongoing research, we notice that fundamentals have deteriorated over the last few earnings reports. Or management was forced to cut the dividend to pay off some debt. Whatever the reason is, if things didn't work out the way we expected, we'd unload our shares and move on to our next idea.

### The company announces an accounting irregularity

This is a tell-tale sign that management is committing fraud. Escape!

## We think we can do better with a different investment

Opportunity cost is always important to consider. If our money is just sitting in a stock that's going nowhere, perhaps it's time to shift gears.

## The company gets acquired

The best time to sell shares is usually right when news of the acquisition breaks. The company being acquired usually sees its shares jump immediately. We can always buy shares of the acquiring company later if we're interested.

## We want cash to support our lifestyle

Maybe we want to take a family vacation or need to pay tuition. Perhaps we want to repair our roof, buy a new car or fly to space with Jeff Bezos.

Investing is about growing your money so you can spend it on the things you want and need. That's the best reason to sell!

---

We don't believe in rebalancing our portfolio. Rebalancing is for mutual funds! Why sell our winners to maintain an arbitrary weighting of each stock in the portfolio?

Suppose a stock has done really well and is taking up an outsized percentage of the portfolio. In that case, we might take some profits and trim some of our position if the opportunity presents itself.

---

# The Most Important Skill

By now, we should better understand the fundamentals of a business and can decide whether we want to own it in our portfolio.

Here's what we've covered:

- ▶ The steps required to select a stock
- ▶ The detective work needed to dig through its financials
- ▶ How to think differently to gain an edge

The ultimate challenge in putting this all together is learning to manage our emotions. This skill requires experience and dedication.

The best way to sharpen that skill is to approach investing with cold logic and a clear-headed view.

Watching a portfolio rise and fall over time without making rash decisions requires patience, discipline, and an ample amount of grit. We can't control the market, but we can control how we respond to its movements.

> ## Don't fall in love with a stock.

Our only goal as an investor is to profit from our investments — we're not rooting for a sports team.

When we take emotion out of our investing decisions, we realize that a stock doesn't know or care that we own it. We don't want to fall in love with a stock so that its deficiencies blind us.

We don't hold on to a loser for too long if the reasons we bought it in the first place are no longer there. We ask ourselves: instead of using free cash wisely, has management made questionable acquisitions? What if a new product, destined to be a blockbuster, turned out to be a dud?

When we sell a stock for a loss, we've acknowledged that we've made a mistake. Most people can't bear to admit they were wrong, so they hold on, hoping to get their money back.

We don't take investing personally. It's far better to learn from a mistake than suffer more significant losses because of an emotional attachment to the company. Sometimes the best course of action is to cut ties, say goodbye and use our cash for a more profitable investment.

We take the same approach when a stock goes up. If we sold some shares and the stock keeps rising, we don't kick ourselves. Instead, we think of this quote by Baron Rothschild: "I made my fortune by selling too early."

# How We Profit From Irrational Behavior

Anyone who claims that humans are rational creatures has never closely followed the stock market!

When a stock with $14 billion in Free Cash Flow drops 10% after narrowly missing quarterly earnings expectations from analysts, does that make any sense?

If the NASDAQ falls 2% and drags Microsoft down with it, why not snatch up some shares at a discount?

Instead of buying stocks on sale, the average investor gets squeamish and sells into the decline, blind to opportunity.

We, however, are intrepid individual investors! We are waiting to pounce with cash on hand, ready to take advantage of foolish and unwarranted overreactions.

When people start stampeding towards the exit, we will be there, calmly aware of the strong fundamentals that will likely cause a future rebound in the share price.

Corrections (defined as a 10% drop) and bear markets (a 20% or more drop) are regular occurrences and signal a healthy market cycle. Preparing our portfolio for inevitable downturns allows us to be even-keeled when others are panicking.

There are no sure things in the stock market, but history tells us that a bull market has followed every bear market!

## Be Knowledgeable

Knowledge is the best defense against harmful emotions. So how do we go about building up our knowledge base?

Financial media (cable news, print and online publications) is valuable when it provides critical news updates and worthwhile opinions. However, it's also good at stirring things up and taking advantage of people's emotions.

Take a look at these financial news headlines:

▶ Here's What $1,000 Invested in Vaccine Stocks Would Be Worth Now

▶ This Graph Shows Why the Stock Market is About to Fall Off a Cliff

▶ Stock Market Crash: Expert Warns Stocks Will Drop Up to 60%

Headlines generate clicks but usually don't offer genuine insight. Predictions are useful for getting attention, but the truth is no one knows what the market will do tomorrow.

This fear of the unknown can cause anxiety, and anxious investors tend to make bad investing decisions. Knowledge and research counteract those unproductive emotions.

That is why we created this Playbook. We've reviewed our core principles, prioritized critical areas of our fundamental research and organized them. This way, we can be as knowledgable about our investments as possible.

In the next section, we'll cover another way that you can benefit from our research and methodology.

# Putting It All Together

Congratulations! You've made it to the end of this Playbook and have completed an in-depth analysis of a company.

We run the analysis on the "Stock Summary" page every fiscal quarter, as numbers constantly change. It's also helpful to save them for historical records.

At American Dream Investing, our investment process begins with this level of detailed analysis.

As we begin to build a position in a stock, one strategy we employ is to not purchase all the desired shares at once. For example, if our goal were to invest $50,000 into a company, we would start by initiating a $25,000 position, waiting and watching the stock's short-term movements before investing more. Here's why:

We want to test our hypothesis to see if we were correct before buying more. The stock could dip in the near-term if there are unforeseen events in the broader market. We would then average down our cost-basis without stretching ourselves and investing more than initially planned.

If the stock rises, it's a good sign we were correct. We can continue adding to the position over time as we gain experience owning the stock and tracking its price movements.

Our success comes from thorough fundamental analysis, monitoring the market and the companies we hold every day, and executing well-developed investment strategies like the one above.

# The Next Stage Of The Journey

Some may think that financial analysis is yawn-inducing, head-scratching and tedious, but we love this kind of work. Finding a missing piece from a breaking news item and tying that to the financial statements is where we can make large amounts of money!

Members of American Dream Investing capitalize on our analysis and decades of experience. We are continuously publishing our exclusive content and commentary.

Even better: we've developed a service for Members to receive **real-time text and email alerts** whenever we make a trade. We peel back the curtain on our portfolio holdings and allocations. We've constructed Model Portfolios based on ours that Members can use to build similar portfolios of different sizes.

Learn About Membership Today

www.americandreaminvesting.com/membership

Our Members find these alerts incredibly helpful. They save time, help them make money and reveal new investing opportunities they may have otherwise missed.

Members know they can rely on us to do the heavy lifting for them with our comprehensive research. The most popular benefit is that Members can be anywhere in the world and receive these alerts without constantly tracking the stock market.

If you'd like to see what we're investing in and be alerted to every trade we make, we invite you to become a member today!

# Glossary of Terms & References

### Cost of Goods Sold (COGS)

All costs associated with the production of the goods sold by a company. These include materials, labor, and manufacturing overhead directly used to create the product. Indirect costs, or those not involved directly in the production of the good, are excluded. A higher COGS results in lower margins.

### Current Ratio

A ratio that measures a company's short-term liquidity. The time frame of "current" signifies within one year. It compares a company's Current Assets to its Current Liabilities that will be earned and paid, respectively, within the next year. The Current Ratio provides insight into the company's ability to cover its short-term debt with its Current Assets.

### Dividends

The distribution of a portion of a company's earnings to shareholders. Typically, a fast-growing company will not pay out dividends, as they reinvest their earnings in continued growth. Dividend-paying companies are almost always well-established companies with a long history of earnings.

### Dividend Yield

The calculation of the total annual dividends divided by the current share price. Income investors often look for higher-yielding stocks when choosing between investment instruments.

### Earnings Per Share

A commonly used ratio that many investors will refer to in a basic overview of a stock. Simply put, it is the Earnings or Net Income divided by the number of Shares Outstanding. While EPS is not enough to make an informed decision regarding investments, it's often used to calculate other valuable ratios.

### Economic Moat

Warren Buffett popularized this term referring to a business's ability to sustain a competitive advantage over competitors to protect its long-term profits and market share.

### Free Cash Flow (FCF)

The cash a company generates after accounting for cash outflows to support operations and maintain its capital assets. FCF can be used to raise dividends, buy back shares, fuel growth, pay down debt, pay interest to investors, and carry forward.

## Guidance

A company's report to shareholders on its expected earnings in the upcoming quarter or year, typically given when the previous quarter's earnings are released. The Guidance will impact the analysts' ratings who cover the stock.

## Market Share

Market Share is the sales amount of a product or service a company makes divided by that item's total sales within an industry, expressed as a percentage.

## Net Income

A calculation of a company's earnings by subtracting expenses from the sales revenue. Net Income is used to calculate Earnings Per Share and is also known as the "Bottom Line" or Net Profit.

## Price to Earnings Ratio (P/E Ratio)

A ratio for valuing a company that takes the current share price and divides it by Earnings Per Share. P/E ratios vary depending on industries, and some companies may not have a ratio if their earnings are negative. Many investors start here in their analysis of a potential investment.

# References

- CNBC.COM
- FINANCE.YAHOO.COM
- GRAHAM, BENJAMIN. THE INTELLIGENT INVESTOR. HARPER BUSINESS, 1973.
- INVESTOPEDIA.COM
- LYNCH, PETER. ONE UP ON WALL STREET. SIMON & SCHUSTER, 1989.
- MORNINGSTAR.COM
- PLEWA, FRANKLIN & FRIEDLOB, GEORGE. UNDERSTANDING CASH FLOW, 1995.
- PODOLNY, JOEL & HANSEN, MORTEN. HARVARD BUSINESS REVIEW, HOW APPLE IS ORGANIZED FOR INNOVATION, NOV-DEC 2020.

# Disclaimer and Disclosure

PAST PERFORMANCE IS NO GUARANTEE OF FUTURE RETURNS. THE MATERIALS AND INFORMATION CONTAINED HEREIN ARE FOR GENERAL INFORMATIONAL PURPOSES ONLY. IN PROVIDING THE INFORMATION IN THIS PUBLICATION, NEITHER KARL KAUFMAN NOR AMERICAN DREAM INVESTING LLC HAVE CONSIDERED YOUR FINANCIAL SOPHISTICATION, FINANCIAL SITUATION, INVESTING TIME HORIZON OR RISK TOLERANCE.

AMERICAN DREAM INVESTING LLC IS NOT A REGISTERED INVESTMENT ADVISER, AND YOU SHOULD NOT CONSIDER ANY INFORMATION HEREIN AS FINANCIAL OR INVESTMENT ADVICE. AUTHOR KARL KAUFMAN IS NOT AN INVESTMENT ADVISER AND DOES NOT ACT AS A FINANCIAL ADVISOR. THE INFORMATION HEREIN IS NOT PERSONALIZED FINANCIAL ADVICE AND IN NO WAY SHOULD BE CONSTRUED AS FINANCIAL ADVICE.

NONE OF THE INFORMATION PROVIDED IN THIS BOOK IS INTENDED AS INVESTMENT, TAX, ACCOUNTING OR LEGAL ADVICE, NOR AS AN OFFER OR SOLICITATION OF AN OFFER TO BUY OR SELL ANY SECURITIES, NOR AS AN ENDORSEMENT, RECOMMENDATION OR SPONSORSHIP OF ANY COMPANY, SECURITY, OR FUND. YOU SHOULD NOT RELY ON THE INFORMATION IN THIS PUBLICATION FOR PURPOSES OF TRANSACTING SECURITIES OR OTHER INVESTMENTS.

YOU ARE SOLELY RESPONSIBLE FOR ANY SECURITIES TRANSACTION YOU ENTER INTO, AND THE PUBLISHERS STRONGLY URGE YOU TO CONSULT TAX, LEGAL, AND/OR FINANCIAL PROFESSIONALS BEFORE ACTING ON ANY INFORMATION PROVIDED HEREIN.

THIS BOOK IS NOT INTENDED AS A PROMOTION OF ANY PARTICULAR PRODUCT OR INVESTMENTS, AND NEITHER KARL KAUFMAN NOR AMERICAN DREAM INVESTING LLC NOR ANY OF THEIR OFFICERS, DIRECTORS, AFFILIATES, EMPLOYEES, AGENTS, OR REPRESENTATIVES IN ANY WAY RECOMMENDS OR ENDORSES ANY COMPANY, PRODUCT, INVESTMENT OR OPPORTUNITY WHICH MAY BE DISCUSSED HEREIN.

THE EDUCATION AND INFORMATION PRESENTED HEREIN IS INTENDED FOR A GENERAL AUDIENCE AND DOES NOT PURPORT TO BE, NOR SHOULD IT BE CONSTRUED AS SPECIFIC ADVICE TAILORED TO ANY INDIVIDUAL. THE PUBLISHERS STRONGLY URGE YOU TO DISCUSS ANY INVESTMENT OPPORTUNITIES WITH YOUR ATTORNEY, ACCOUNTANT, FINANCIAL PROFESSIONAL AND/OR OTHER ADVISOR. YOUR USE OF THE INFORMATION CONTAINED HEREIN IS AT YOUR OWN RISK.

THE CONTENT IS PROVIDED 'AS IS' AND WITHOUT WARRANTIES OF ANY KIND, EITHER EXPRESSED OR IMPLIED. AMERICAN DREAM INVESTING LLC AND KARL KAUFMAN HEREBY DISCLAIM ALL WARRANTIES, INCLUDING BUT NOT LIMITED TO: ANY IMPLIED WARRANTIES OF MERCHANTABILITY, FITNESS FOR A PARTICULAR PURPOSE, TITLE, OR NON-INFRINGEMENT. NEITHER KARL KAUFMAN NOR AMERICAN DREAM INVESTING LLC PROMISES OR GUARANTEES ANY PARTICULAR RESULT FROM YOUR USE OF THE INFORMATION CONTAINED HEREIN.

NEITHER KARL KAUFMAN NOR AMERICAN DREAM INVESTING LLC ASSUME ANY LIABILITY OR RESPONSIBILITY FOR ERRORS OR OMISSIONS IN THE INFORMATION CONTAINED HEREIN. KARL KAUFMAN WILL NOT BE LIABLE FOR ANY INCIDENTAL, DIRECT, INDIRECT, PUNITIVE, ACTUAL, CONSEQUENTIAL, SPECIAL, EXEMPLARY, OR OTHER DAMAGES, INCLUDING, BUT NOT LIMITED TO, LOSS OF REVENUE OR INCOME, PAIN AND SUFFERING, EMOTIONAL DISTRESS, OR SIMILAR DAMAGES, EVEN IF HE HAS BEEN ADVISED OF THE POSSIBILITY OF SUCH DAMAGES. IN NO EVENT WILL THE COLLECTIVE LIABILITY OF AMERICAN DREAM INVESTING TO ANY PARTY (REGARDLESS OF THE FORM OF ACTION, WHETHER IN CONTRACT, TORT, OR OTHERWISE) EXCEED THE GREATER OF $100 OR THE AMOUNT YOU HAVE PAID FOR THE INFORMATION, PRODUCT OR SERVICE OUT OF WHICH LIABILITY AROSE. UNDER NO CIRCUMSTANCES WILL KARL KAUFMAN BE LIABLE FOR ANY LOSS OR DAMAGE CAUSED BY YOUR RELIANCE ON THE INFORMATION CONTAINED HEREIN.

IT IS YOUR RESPONSIBILITY TO EVALUATE THE ACCURACY, COMPLETENESS OR USEFULNESS OF ANY INFORMATION, OPINION, ADVICE OR OTHER CONTENT CONTAINED HEREIN. PLEASE SEEK THE ADVICE OF PROFESSIONALS, AS APPROPRIATE, REGARDING THE EVALUATION OF ANY SPECIFIC INFORMATION, OPINION, ADVICE OR OTHER CONTENT. DO NOT INTERPRET THE EXAMPLES IN THESE MATERIALS AS A PROMISE OR GUARANTEE OF EARNINGS. ANY CLAIMS MADE OF ACTUAL EARNINGS OR EXAMPLES OF ACTUAL RESULTS WILL BE VERIFIED UPON REQUEST.

# Notes

# Notes

# Notes

# Notes

# Notes